Write On!

Write On!

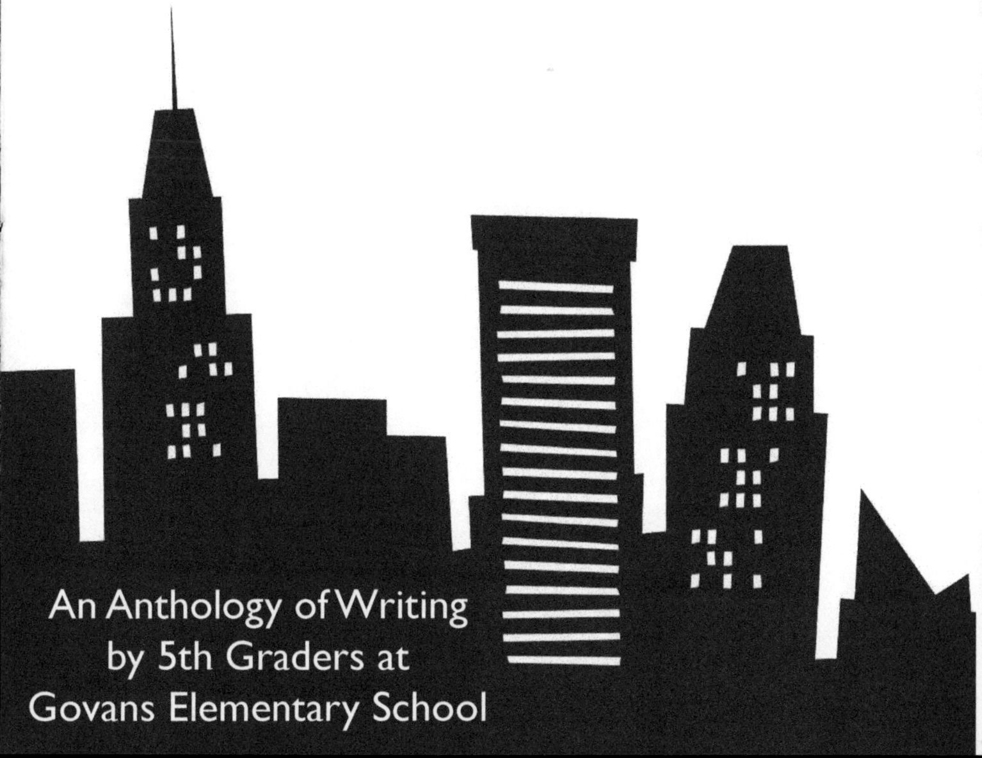

An Anthology of Writing
by 5th Graders at
Govans Elementary School

© 2012, CityLit Project

ISBN: 978-1-936328-10-9
CityLit Project is a 501(c)(3) nonprofit organization
with offices in the School of Communications Design
at the University of Baltimore.
Federal Tax ID Number: 20-0639118

All rights reserved. No part of this book may be
reproduced or transmitted in any form or by any means,
electronic or mechanical, including photocopy, recording,
or any information storage and retrieval system,
without prior permission from the publisher
(except by reviewers who may quote brief passages).

Printed in the United States of America | First Edition
CityLit Kids photograph: Lauren Beck
Book design: Lauren Beck and Gregg Wilhelm

c/o CityLit Project
120 S. Curley Street
Baltimore, MD 21224
410.274.5691
www.CityLitProject.org
info@citylitproject.org

This book is dedicated to Ms. O'Keefe.

Table of Contents

9	Introduction
11	Party Time
13	Cake's Fortune
15	Welcome to My Hood
17	Summer Time
19	The Ghost
21	Where the Wild Things Are
23	Friends
25	The First Day of Spring
27	Snow Hood and Red Hood
29	Jordan in a Loony Toons Cartoon
31	Simile Poem
33	The Report Card's Treat
35	This is Just to Say
37	Mischief of Fortune
39	Who Knew?
41	Goldiey Locks and the Four Bears
43	Math Touch
45	Spring and Summer Fun
47	Snow Pink
49	Fame of Fortune
51	Starlight
53	My Brother has a Crazy Imaginary Friend
55	My Room Is Inside Out
57	Mean Girls
59	Cinderella and the Secret Friend
61	About the Authors
65	About CityLit Kids

Introduction

As the 2011–12 school year draws to a close, the fifth-grade participants in the CityLit Kids program at Govans Elementary might take a look at their journals and notice that they have been very prolific this year. Over twenty-seven class sessions, they've explored elements of fiction and poetry, such as character, suspense, imagery, desire, and conflict, and they've experimented with several poetic forms. Most importantly, they've learned the importance—and power—of revision.

Write On! offers a sampling of the fifth-graders' hard work, and especially the rewards of revision. Contained in it are haikus, apology poems, fairy tale adaptations, adventures, tall tales, and earnest expressions of love, friendship, struggles, and humor. The book represents only a fraction of the effort and strong thinking that bubbled up in Ms. O'Keefe's classroom as the CityLit kids listened, learned, wrote, and shared.

As the CityLit Kids co-founders and teachers, we have been impressed by these students' growth as creative readers and writers over the previous two years. We have been touched by their enthusiasm, and by their willingness to stretch their minds and try things that feel difficult at first. We hope that they will carry with them throughout their education the sense of adventure and bravery that they brought to their writing in the program.

—Miss Christine, Miss Elisabeth, Miss Elissa, Miss Jane, and Miss Liz

Party Time
by Autumn Aaron

A girl named Kelis had a sister and a brother and her mother passed away when she was five. Now she is twelve, and I am her best friend, almost sister. Her father was going on vacation, so she had to watch her sister and brother for two weeks. She said, "For how much?" 150 dollars. As soon as her father left, I called and we had the house to ourselves for two weeks and it was fun.

Cake's Fortune
by Kayla Blackwell

Once upon a time, there was a girl named Cake. One day a man saw Cake and her cow so Cake traded the family cow for three magic eggs. When Cake got home her mom was very angry.

She yelled, "Where have you been and where is the cow?"

Cake said, "I traded her for these magic eggs."

"You wha…what is that noise?" Cake's mom opened the door and she saw people coming, saying they would give her money.

"O…m….g," said Cake's mom. A man came out and said he would give her one thousand dollars for those eggs. Then a woman came and said she would give her one million dollars for those eggs. So they traded the eggs in for the money. Cake actually stole the money from them and ran off with the eggs. Cake went to California where her friend Sasha lived. Cake said she would give Sasha five thousand dollars if she didn't say anything to anybody about her being there.

"I am going to the mall. Sasha, can I trust you too look after my money?"

"Of course I can," said Sasha.

When Cake left, Sasha took the money and the eggs. When Cake got back she said she had bought some purses for Sasha. Cake went into the other room and the money, the eggs and Sasha were gone. Cake looked in the master room. Sasha was there. Cake smacked Sasha in the face.

Sasha said, "I was just putting your money in a safer place."

Cake said, "Where are the eggs?"

"In the bathroom."

"No they're not," Cake said.

There was also a broken window.

Welcome to My Hood
by Deairra Brandon

There was a little girl in Cinderella Hood named Cinderella who wanted to visit her grandmother because she hadn't seen her in a long time. Her mother let her go visit her grandmother. As Cinderella was walking through the woods in the hood smelling the flowers, a wolf stopped her out of nowhere. The wolf asked her where she was heading to and Cinderella said, "Over the bridge to my grandmother's house."

The wolf said, "Oh really? What's her address? I would like to visit her."

"1130 Druid Hill Drive."

After Cinderella told the wolf the address, he ran over the bridge but Cinderella didn't know where he was going. When she got there, he wasn't there. The whole time, the wolf had eaten the grandmother.

Summer Time
by Taylor Cooper

Summer is fun,
Summer is great,
Summer is a time to celebrate.
Go to the pool and splash around,
Your mom calls you to go to the playground.
You had fun,
To splash and play
The sun goes down,
Can't wait until the next day!

The Ghost
by Kerel Davidson

John said, "Did you hear something in the attic?"

Chris said, "No." John told Chris to follow him.

John said, "Ready?"

As John went into the attic, Chris said, "There's a ghost!"

The ghost said, "Leave and never return."

John said, "No, this is our home."

The ghost got mad and said, "You had your chance. Now you die." As the ghost flew over, it pushed Chris out the window while a train was coming.

John yelled "Chriiiiiiissssssssssss!"

The ghost said, "This is the end!"

John jumped out the window and caught Chris. Then they landed on the train and the ghost flew out the window, and flew through Chris and took his soul and he falls off the train. Another ghost comes and kills the evil ghost and then goes away.

Where the Wild Things Are
by Elisha Davis

Once upon a time, there was a boy named Jordan. One night while he was asleep, he heard a loud bang.

"What was that?" he said.

He grabbed his metal bat to go investigate. That was one of the worst things he could have done. He went to the kitchen and turned on the light and then he saw him. It was a big, hairy, nasty looking ugly man. He threw the bat at his head to knock him out, but it just made him angry. Jordan ran upstairs as fast as he could, grabbed his baby sister and brother and went to his parents' room and locked the door. He woke his parents. They were frightened. Everyone in the house was awake. The guy left. The family took a sigh of relief.

Jordan went downstairs to find nothing damaged or missing except some ham, bread, mayo, cheese, chips and Kool-aid. Jordan grabbed his bat and went to his room. He could not sleep, so he thought happy thoughts while snuggling with his bat. He got deeper into his thoughts until he was gone from reality. He was in Imagination Land.

In Imagination Land, he was with the love of his life. Then he started seeing fourteen-legged monsters and then he said to the love of his life, "This is not imagination land anymore, baby. This is where the wild things are!"

And that's where the story begins.

Friends
by Jubre Edwards

Trust is friends that laugh,
Trust is friends that play.
Trust is friends that keep secrets,
And believe everything you say.
Trust is friends that fight,
And share tears together.
Then be friends when they feel
They miss each other.

The First Day of Spring
by Justice Georgie

Trees are evolving
beautifully, as spring sets
wonders in the
sky
as the day blooms
not another
goes by

Snow Hood and Red Hood
by Alexandria Goslee

Once upon a time, there were two friends, Little Snow Hood and Little Red Hood. They were best friends since they were born. One day, they were walking home from school and said, "Let's have a mansion sleepover." Little Red said yes. Then they sang their special song:

> *Boo yea, it's alright*
> *Let's go take a hike*
> *Boom, baby (clap)*

So they went to each other's house to get ready. Then they took a hike in the woods and found a mansion next to grandma's. So they went inside. Little did they know it was grandpapa wolf's and they had went to bed. Five hours later, they awoke to a strange noise and it was grandpapa and his boys, back from eating a hearty meal. They ran in the closet for eight days. And they ran out and went to grandma's and grandpapa was in their bed saying, "Deary, come here!" They ran upstairs and then out he jumped, but they ran down the stairs and out of the house.

Jordan in a Loony Tunes Cartoon
by Ebony Hendricks

Jordan was the shyest kid in school. He had to write a five page essay on what he was going to do for spring break. Jordan and his mom went into a place called Loony Toons cartoon and they jumped into the television and they had to meet Daffy Duck, Bugs Bunny and Porky Pig. And then, when Jordan went back to school and read his essay, the whole class got up and clapped loudly.

Simile Poem
by Jabriea Johnson

The walls are as bright as the lights on a car.
The lights are as long as a long line of people.
The flag is like a colorful picture.
The classroom is as big as a house.
The sky is as blue as my eyes.
The board is as still as a mannequin.
The TV is as black as her earrings.

The Report Card's Treat
by Lamont Jones

Once there was a boy named Shawn. Shawn wanted to go to Six Flags. His mother said if he got a good report card he could go.

The next day, when Shawn walked to school and into his classroom, he read what was on the blackboard: Report cards will given out at the end of the week. When class started, Shawn grabbed his warm-up and did it. He got all of the questions right. After the warm-up, he did his math test. Shawn got all the questions on his test right. At the end of the day, Shawn's teacher gave him a certificate that said, Congratulations, you got everything you did right.

When Shawn went home he did his homework, studied, played his game, then went to sleep. The next day, Shawn did the same thing he did yesterday, got everything right, did his homework, studied, played his game, and went to sleep. Shawn did this same thing for the rest of the week.

When Shawn got his report card, he had all As. Shawn got to go to Six Flags, and he had a ball at the water park.

This is Just to Say
by Taylor Jones

Sorry I stole the ice cream that day. It was so good and creamy. The vanilla stain on my shirt gave me away.

It's Okay, Catie

Okay Catie, I see that you ate the old ice cream that has been in the freezer for the three weeks. So you are going to be sick.

Mischief of Fortune
by Jaylon Judd

Jack Condor was a mischievious boy. He always played tricks on people. He always got 50s and under on his grades. One day at school, he put glue on the teacher's chair and she had to get surgery to get it off.

One day, while he was walking home, Jack saw a fortune teller booth on the sidewalk. He went over to it and asked the man if could get his fortune. The man gave him a card and it said that he would cause mischief all over the world. Then Jack felt a tingling pain coming from his back. Then two wings sprouted from his back and flew up in the air and caused mischief. He went high in the air and never came down.

Moral of the story: If you cause trouble, trouble will come to you.

Who Knew?
by Alain Kibet

"Jordan, where's the box for my bedroom?" Jordan's mom said. Jordan is the shyest kid in town. He just moved from Seattle to Austin, Texas. He went inside with his mother and went to play his video game while his mother and father unpacked their boxes. The next day, he went to eat breakfast. He entered the kitchen and saw his mother had cooked his favorite meal of bacon, eggs and orange juice. His mother reminded him that night was family conference. Every Friday night, they talk about what they did that week. Mainly, his sister showed her art. Sometimes she drew the *Mona Lisa* or Blue Boy.

"Thanks for breakfast!"

Jordan left home with a full stomach to go to school to enroll.

"You have a pretty good record. I am going to put you in the advanced program."

As he went to class, he thought "What should I represent in the family conference?" Suddenly, something came to his mind. He could join the basketball team because his father always wanted to see his son in a basketball game. His sister showed her art, and he showed his basketball. For the first time, he won the family conference.

Goldiey Locks and the Four Bears

by Nasia Lawton

Once there was a family of four bears, father bear, mother bear, Aunty bear and Junior bear. Aunty bear loved a show called "Goldiey Locks it Up" that's about a girl named Goldiey Locks redesigning people's homes.

So one day, Junior bear came home from school and made a video about how messed up their house was and sent it in to Goldiey Locks to redesign their house. So mother and father came home from work. Mother cooked dinner. It was called porridge and it's close to oatmeal. They went to bed. Then the next morning they all left going on about their day.

While they were gone, Goldiey Locks came to redecorate. The house was made out of all candy. Father bear was a fisher and hadn't caught any fish that day. Mother bear was trying out for Neverland's Best Talent Show, and was eliminated. And Junior bear got embarrassed in front of his crush in school. So they all had a bad day. They all finally got home.

"Surprise!" Junior bear shouted. "Mom and dad, I sent in a video so Goldiey Locks could redesign our house."

Suddenly, Junior bear had to go to the bathroom. He heard something buzzing. He opened the window and it was bees. They attacked everyone. They had to clean up the mess. They wanted their old house back except for the kitchen and the flat screen. Later, Goldiey Locks's manager set up a reality show for Goldiey Locks and the Four Bears.

Math Touch

by Xavier Shipp

It was a dark and stormy night, and this boy named Jason was at his house on the computer Googling vampires because all of his "friends" said that they're not real. But Jason ignored them. Well, he tried. Everybody still teased him. So he invented the "Math Touch." He would touch Mr. Wickerson, the sixth grade math teacher. Yeah, it was stupid, but everybody played it. Even Mrs. Wickerson. When Mr. Wickerson found out, it wasn't a pretty picture. But when he told Mrs. Wickerson, she said "I will…"

Spring and Summer Fun (A Haiku)
by Misha Smith

Sneezing, itching eyes
apple, mango, oranges, fruit
swimming, fun, playing

Snow Pink

by Kaiyana Spivey

Once there was a girl named Snow Pink. She had seven sisters. They got on her nerves. Their names were Snow Orange, Snow Yellow, Snow White, Snow Green (my favorite), Snow Blue, Snow Red and Snow Purple. They got on her nerves a lot.

Snow Pink was only thirteen, but she wanted to go to her best friend's party. So she went downstairs and started talking.

"Mom, can I please go to this new party in Pikesville? Please?"

"No!" her mom said.

"But why?"

"You know what? You can go but you better be in this house by 11 pm!"

"Okay, ma!"

Fame of Fortune
by Kenyan Stevenson

My character wants to grow up and be famous and dance. She said that when that day comes, she is going to have the most money of all. My character is named Beaty and now Beaty says that she loves her job and she is happy that she followed her dream. Beaty said that she is making more money than she made when she was working at the Goodwill.

Starlight
by Kyurn Taylor

Moon shines well with the stars
The party starts wherever we are
Lambo's, Ferrari, all types of cars
I don't need the key, I press start
What I am explaining is my life
It shines bright like a night
I live my life fast like the types of cars
And I don't need the key, I press start

My Brother has a Crazy Imaginary Friend
by Sade Tenabe

One day my brother and I were on our way out the door when he called mom and said Chris and Kendall were going to catch the bus. Then mom came downstairs patting her head.

"Who is Chris?" she said.

Then my brother said, "Chris is my friend."

Then things started to happen. I saw him. I asked Kameel if his friend had on gray sweat pants, blue shell heads and a Ravens jersey. Then Kameel said yes. I pulled out my phone to call 911 when Chris typed in youtube.com. I was scared. Then he put on *Asking All Them Questions*. My phone finally called 911. Then they came and took me to crazy jail.

My Room Is Inside Out
by Danaya Thomas

I'm just an ordinary kid named Jock who was mad at my mother for sending me to my room for feeding my vegetables to my cat named Whiskers. So when I drank my orange soda, all of a sudden my room turned into Candyland, and I started eating candy. I met a man named Mr. Peppermint and he told me to join the pepper side and I said no! And then, I started to miss my mom and then I said, "There's no place like home" and then Candyland turned back into my room. Then I apologized and Mommy said, "I accept your apology." And then we hugged and I said, "Wow, my room is inside out!"

Mean Girls
by Destini Thrweatt

Once there was a girl named Lizy. She was the diva dash at school with her two friends Kate and Christy. They ruled Way Bay High. The other students called them the populars. They were always mean to people.

But one day, before the big dance her parents said she couldn't go because she knew her teacher's name was Ms. Pants, but her teacher called and said a student told on her for calling Ms. Pants "Lacy face, makes a great paste," and said that it had been her third strike already.

"Mom, Dad, I only said that because she wouldn't let me do my nails in class and she wears her pants up to her neck."

"That was rude to say," said Mom.

So she snuck out and went to the dance and got wet guacamole poured on her. That was payback, or probably karma. The next day her friend Jacob said, "Do you want to go to prom with me on Saturday?"

She said, "Sure but I am grounded because of the teacher and that girl that told on me."

So she walked away and then the girl said,

"Make way two times for the populars." She was so rude to people, this was going on her record. She smashed people's books on the ground and poured coffee in everyone's hair. It was like a cat learning how to fly or being a first lady.

So Kate said, "Someone just asked me to prom and I sad yes." Then we went to KFC for chicken.

Cinderella and the Secret Friend

by Raven Ware

Cinderella was a girl with two evil step sisters. They even had magic powers. They used them to upset Cinderella.

One day, Cinderella grew wings and with those wings she left that house. She flew to the gold forest which was not even gold. As she walked in the woods, she saw a girl. The girl was in red jeans with a light red vest with a shirt with words that read "You got the reds." So Cinderella said hi to the girl. Then the girl said, "Hi. My name is Teenage Red."

Cinderella said, "Weird name."

Teenage Red said, "So is Cinderella. I'll call you Cinder."

"And I'll call you Reds."

Then Reds said, "There's a castle that way."

"Which way?" said Cinderella.

"The way you just came from."

"Don't remind me. I live there."

"Really? Then let's go there."

"No, Reds. If you go there, then my sisters will turn you into a frog. Just like the rest."

"Okay, Cinder, we won't go. But where are we going to go?"

"Anywhere else!"

Then they went and lived their lives with going into that castle.

About the Authors

Autum Aaron is the author of "Party Time" and she likes books.

Kayla Blackwell is the author of "Cake's Fortune." She is ten years old and loves to read. Kayla is very kind and has many friends.

Deairra Brandon is the author of "Welcome to My Hood." She has been writing since she was in the third grade. She loves dancing and reading books.

Taylor Cooper is the author of "Summer Time." She likes to sing and dance and write stories.

Kerel Davidson is the author of "The Ghost." He is eleven years old. He likes playing video games, watching television, and playing outside with his little brother. Kerel is a Capricorn and was born on January 22nd.

Elisha C. Davis is the author of "Where the Wild Things Are." He is an educated young man. He is eleven years old and in the fifth grade. Elisha has sadly lost both of his parents. His birthday is November 13th. He says, "When I grow up, I want to get my master's degree, Ph.D., a degree in cooking and in teaching." Elisha is going to Baltimore Design School for middle school, and hopes to go to Baltimore Polytechnic Institute for high school

Jubre Edwards is the author of "Friends." She loves animals and nature. She believes that family always comes first, but she still loves her friends, which inspired her piece that appears in this book.

Justice Georgie is the author of "The First Day of Spring." He is a charismatic young man. The next time you see him, he will be a well paid WWE entertainer. If not that, he will be a successful actor.

Alexandria Goslee is the author of "Snow Hood and Red Hood." She is from Salisbury, Maryland. She loves to swim, dance and play outside. She loves to have fun with her cousins and her best friends.

Ebony Hendricks is the author of "Jordan in a Loony Toons Cartoon." She likes to ride really high roller coasters. She likes to go to the pool and the beach. Her favorite colors are ebony, ivory, green and blue.

Jabriea Johnson is the author of "Simile Poem." She is a very smart girl. She loves to listen to music. She wants to be a math teacher or college professor one day.

Lamont Jones is the author of "The Report Card's Treat." He is a fifth grader at Govans Elementary School.

Taylor Jones is the author of "This is Just to Say" and "It's Okay, Catie." She is from Princeton, New Jersey. She is eleven years old. Her favorite colors are red, green, purple and light blue.

Jaylon Judd is the author of "Mischief of Fortune." He likes to play video games and exercise with his family. He likes to eat pizza and fast food. He has a cat and two dogs that he loves very much. He has a brother and sister and likes to go on vacation to visit other places.

Alain Kibet is the author of "Who Knew?" He is smart and intelligent. He loves music and his favorite color is purple. His role model is Ben Carson.

Nasia Lawton is the author of "Goldiey Locks and the Four Bears." She is eleven years old and in the fifth grade. She is African American and Korean. She enjoys Korean food and traditions. She hopes to one day become a lawyer, teacher or hairstylist. She was born in Maryland. She started writing stories and poems in third grade and will continue to write.

Xavier Shipp is the author of "Math Touch." He enjoys playing sports. When he grows up, he wants to be a doctor.

Misha Smith is the author of "Spring and Summer Fun." She is eleven years old and in the fifth grade. She has strong qualities and good grades. When she grows up she wants to be a scientist because she loves science. She would also like to be an author.

Kaiyana Spivey is the author of "Snow Pink." She is from Brooklyn, New York. Her favorite colors are pink, green, white and black.

Kenyan Stevenson is the author of "The Fame of Fortune." Kenyan loves books and loves to read.

Kyurn Taylor is the author of "Starlight." He is ten years old and is a good person once you get to know him.

Sade Tenabe is the author of "My Brother has a Crazy Imaginary Friend." Sade lives next to her grandmother and her crazy dog. Every time she rides her bike, the dog chases her away and then they are both out of breath.

Danaya Thomas is the author of "My Room Is Inside Out." She is ten years old. Her birthday is March 5th. She is very fashionable and has many friends.

Destini M. Thrweatt is the author of "Mean Girls." She is an intelligent girl in the fifth grade. She loves to write and design. Her goals are to become a designer or a chef. She means well to everyone.

Raven Ware is the author of "Cinderella and the Secret Friend." She is in fifth grade. When she grows up, she wants to be a famous singer.

About CityLit Kids

CityLit Kids builds a community of enthusiastic readers and writers in Baltimore City public schools by bringing the literary community into the classroom. Operating currently at Govans Elementary, the program works with fourth- and fifth-graders to explore aspects of creative writing through read-aloud activities, creative journaling, guest visits by local authors, and short- and long-term writing projects.

Over the course of the school year, students in the program become excited about creative writing and build confidence in their own ability to write and think creatively. Through CityLit Kids, a community of readers and writers is born, populated by pupils, teachers, volunteers, and guest writers. Students are encouraged to share their ideas and their work, and they are challenged to write and think in ways that may be new to them. The school year ends with a celebration: teachers, pupils, and their families gather to share other's work. In fourth grade, every participating pupil receives copies of the books read over the course of the academic year, as well as a published version of one of their stories or poems. In fifth grade, participants receive a published book showcasing their own writing.

Conceived in the spring of 2010 by co-founders Jane Delury, Christine Grillo, and Elissa Weissman—all writers and educators—CityLit Kids launched in the 2010–2011 school year. Along with interns from the University of Baltimore, the three co-founders provide all of the classroom instruction; the co-founders continuously develop and refine the curriculum. CityLit Kids is a program that operates in partnership with CityLit Project, a Baltimore-based, literary nonprofit organization.

CityLit Kids thanks the University of Baltimore graduate student interns who worked diligently with the program during this school year: Lauren Beck, Tracy Gnadinger, Emily Lee, Christina Lengyel, Lori Miller, and Ashley Payne.

CityLit Kids thanks the University of Baltimore for funding faculty work on the program through a Baltimore Renaissance Seed Scholars Fund grant. The program also thanks the Lockhart Vaughan Foundation, the Lois and Philip Macht Family Philanthropic Fund, and Target for their generous support.

www.ingramcontent.com/pod-product-compliance
Lightning Source LLC
Chambersburg PA
CBHW032215040426
42449CB00005B/600